A Devil and Her Love Song

Story & Art by

Miyoshi Tomori

Volume 1

A Devil and Her Love Song

Volume 1

CONTENTS

WOBBLE
WOBBLE
ZZZZ...
IT'S HARD TO DESCRIBE MARIA EXACTLY.
THAT GIRL FROM ST. KATRIA IS AWFUL.
LOOK AT HER!
KA-CHUNK
KA-CHUNK
THAT OLD LADY'S STANDING RIGHT IN FRONT OF HER...
WOBBLE
KA-CHUNK
IT'S NOT BECAUSE I'M STUPID. (BUT YEAH, THAT COULD BE A FACTOR.)
KA-CHUNK
...BUT SHE'S JUST SITTING THERE.
PRETTY GIRLS ARE USUALLY UGLY INSIDE.
KA-CHUNK

WHAT KIND OF GIRL IS MARIA KAWAI...?

SHE'S A DEVIL.

YOKOHAMA. YOKOHAMA.
YOKOHAMA
SHUP
PLEASE WATCH YOUR STEP AS YOU EXIT.
ZZZ...
FWUMP
SHA
THWAK
?!
W- WHAT'RE YOU-?
twitch
TCH.
YOUR LEG WAS IN MY WAY.
OH, SORRY ...

YOU MUST BE A LOUSY PICKPOCKET IF YOU'RE TARGETING A SLEEPING MAN, YOU OLD CROOK.
WSP
I...
I DON'T KNOW WHAT YOU'RE TALKING ABOUT.
FWSH
flinch
YOU PETTY THIEF.
whew
PETTY...

HOW DID SHE KNOW?
Totsuka High School
"BELIEVE AND YOU SHALL BE SAVED."
THE SISTERS PREACHED THAT MESSAGE CONSTANTLY.
...
TMP
BUT IT'S A LIE. THE TRUTH IS THE TRUTH, WHETHER YOU BELIEVE IT OR NOT.
Amazing grace...

BELIEF HAS NO EFFECT ON HOW PEOPLE SEE YOU.
HEY, SHIN! DID YOU HEAR? WE'RE GETTING A NEW STUDENT TODAY.
How sweet the sound...
OH, HER.
THAT GIRL WHO GOT EXPELLED FROM ST. KATRIA.
Mor-ning, Yusu-ke! ♡
Morning!
SHE MUST BE PRETTY SMART.
WHY'S SHE COMING TO A DEAD-END SCHOOL LIKE OURS?
...that saved a wretch like me...
lift
WHEN YOU SAY GOODBYE TO SOMEONE, THE TRUTH COMES OUT.
ON THE DAY I GOT EXPELLED, I WAS TOLD...

"YOU TAINT EVERY-ONE AROUND YOU."
BANG
I'M MARIA KAWAI.

MUR-MUR
WOW... BEING THAT CUTE SHOULD BE ILLEGAL.
MUR-MUR
THAT'S A ST. KATRIA GIRL, ALL RIGHT.
MUR-MUR
CHECK OUT HER FIGURE.
MUR-MUR
UN-REAL...
MUR-MUR
WHAT'S THAT GOT TO DO WITH ANYTHING? YOU GUYS ARE SO STUPID.
MUR-MUR
LOOK HOW TINY HER FACE IS!
SHE'S SO THIN.
ARE YOU SURE SHE WAS EXPELLED? WHAT FOR?
BETCHA IT WAS A SEX SCANDAL.
HI THERE!
klat
THERE'S A FREE SEAT OVER HERE–
IT WAS AN ACT OF VIOLENCE.

I GOT EXPELLED FOR BEATING UP A TEACHER.
SILENCE...
?
YOU WANTED TO KNOW, DIDN'T YOU?
IF YOU TALK THAT LOUDLY, IT SOUNDS LIKE YOU WANT AN ANSWER.
HEY...
WE DIDN'T MEAN-
OR DID YOU NEED MORE TIME TO GOSSIP FIRST?
AW, RELAX.

YOU JUST GOT HERE. LET'S START OVER.
MY NAME'S YUSUKE KANDA. CALL ME YUSUKE!
IF YOU'VE GOT ANY QUESTIONS, JUST ASK ME, MARIA!
OH, DON'T WORRY.
YOU DON'T HAVE TO KEEP AN EYE ON ME. I'M NOT HERE TO CAUSE TROUBLE.
I CAN TELL YOU'RE NOT REALLY A PEOPLE PERSON. YOU DON'T HAVE TO FORCE YOURSELF TO TALK TO ME.
FROZEN
MUR-MUR
WHAT ...?
IS YUSUKE REALLY LIKE THAT?
SHE'S JUST TRYING TO SOUND CLEVER.
...

I'M UPBEAT! I'M FUN! EVERYBODY LOVES YUSUKE!
THAT'S HOW YOU ARE ON THE SURFACE.
HOW DID SHE KNOW ?!!
Don't be like that. I'm doing my best!
I DON'T KNOW WHAT TO MAKE OF HER.
WAS THAT A LUCKY GUESS, OR IS SHE REALLY INTUITIVE?
CAN SHE EVEN TELL WHETHER SHE'S RIGHT OR NOT?
SHE'S EITHER BEING MALICIOUS OR THOUGHT-FUL.
WHICHEVER IT IS, I WANT NOTHING TO DO WITH HER.

SHIN, WHY DO YOU ALWAYS WRITE PEOPLE OFF LIKE THAT?
YUSUKE KANDA
I HATE PEOPLE WHO GO STRAIGHT FOR THE JUGULAR!
SHIN MEGURO
YOU'RE ALWAYS SO NEGATIVE.
LOOK AT HER... SHE'S ALL ALONE!
And it's only her first day.

I NEED TO BUY A UNIFORM. WHERE'S THE STUDENT STORE?
HUH? YOU'RE ASKING ME?
MAKE UP YOUR MIND.
JUST A MINUTE AGO, YOU TOLD HIM NOT TO TALK TO YOU.
YOU'RE RIGHT. SORRY.
YOU JUST SEEM LIKE THE TYPE WHO THINKS YOU SHOULD BE HELPFUL EVEN WHEN IT'S INCONVENIENT FOR YOU.
I TOOK ADVANTAGE OF THAT.
I'LL FIND IT MYSELF.
WAIT!!
LEAP

I'LL TAKE YOU THERE.
SOOOO, MARIA.
YOU SURE ARE BLUNT. HOW COME?
LIKE, WHY TELL US YOU'RE VIOLENT?
NO ONE WOULD'VE KNOWN IF YOU HADN'T SAID ANYTHING, BUT NOW PEOPLE THINK BADLY OF YOU.
I'VE BEEN TOLD THAT I TAINT PEOPLE.
HUH?
SO I SHOULDN'T HIDE HOW TAINTED I AM.
IT WOULDN'T BE FAIR.

BUT NO ONE CARES ABOUT THAT.
EVEN IF YOU'RE REALLY HORRIBLE INSIDE, WHO WANTS TO SEE IT?
EVERYTHING IN THE WORLD IS BETTER IF YOU FRAME IT RIGHT—YOUR CLOTHES, YOUR MAKEUP, YOUR ROOM, EVEN YOUR LUNCH.
THE SAME GOES FOR GETTING ALONG WITH PEOPLE.
THAT THING YOU SAID TO ME, ABOUT HOW I'M NOT A PEOPLE PERSON?
THAT REALLY HURT.
It almost killed me inside.
BUT IT STINGS LESS IF YOU PUT A LOVELY SPIN ON IT.

"Don't act so nice if you don't like me. I'll get the wrong impression."
FWUFF
AND THEN YOU TILT YOUR HEAD LIKE THIS.
CUTE LITTLE BOW
LOOKING UP AT SOMEONE IS GOOD.
THE EXACT OPPOSITE OF HOW YOU'RE LOOKING DOWN.
...
BUT THAT'S NOT HOW I FEEL.
SO WHAT?
IF YOU DO IT THAT WAY, I WON'T BE OFFENDED...
...AND I'D STILL KNOW YOU WANT TO BE LEFT ALONE.
Store
Store
MISSION ACCOMPLISHED!

IT DOESN'T MATTER IF IT'S TRUE OR NOT, SEE?
WHEN I GOT EXPELLED, ONE OF THE SISTERS SAID...
"YOU'RE INCREDIBLY INTUITIVE, AND THAT MAKES YOU UNIQUE.
CHAK
OH, YEAH. THAT GIRL.

"BUT YOU SEE SO CLEARLY...
"...THAT YOU DRIVE PEOPLE INTO A CORNER, EVEN WHEN YOU DON'T MEAN TO."
MARIA KAWAI!
I SAW HER ON THE TRAIN THIS MORNING.
SHE WAS HORRIBLE.
SHE WOULDN'T GIVE UP HER SEAT...
...AND SHE KICKED A SLEEPING MAN ON HER WAY OFF THE TRAIN.
No way...
That's scary.
Who does that?
AND SHE LEANED OVER AND TOLD AN OLD WOMAN TO DROP DEAD.
Right in her ear.
CHAK
TWITCH
ACTUALLY, YOU'VE GOT IT WRONG.

THAT OLD LADY IS A PICKPOCKET. SHE WAS GOING TO ROB THAT MAN.
THAT'S WHY I WOKE HIM UP.
THAT'S RIDICU-LOUS.
YOU'RE MAKING THAT UP.
NO, IT'S THE TRUTH.
BUT... BUT...
YOU DIDN'T HAVE TO KICK HIM!
RIGHT?
Yeah!
Yeah!
OR TELL HER TO DROP DEAD.
OH... THEY DON'T CARE WHAT HAPPENED.
THEY JUST WANT TO PICK A FIGHT.
NO WONDER THEY'RE NOT LISTENING.
Right?
Yeah!
I don't buy it.
A LOVELY SPIN...
AH...
WHAT?

I may be horrible sometimes, but it's nice to meet you. ♡
Tilt
At just the right angle
TMP
TMP
Eee
THIS "LOVELY" THING IS HARD...
ZWAK
FREEZE
BUT...

...IF I'M HERE FOR A REASON...
FWIP
...SOMEONE WHO DOESN'T TAINT PEOPLE.
...MAYBE ...
I CHANGED...
...I CAN BECOME...
I CHANGED MY UNIFORM.
THIS SAILOR LOOK IS CUTE.

DOES IT LOOK GOOD ON ME?
SILENCE
SHIN...
mumble
NO, IT DOESN'T.
THAT'S MEAN!
IT LOOKS NICE, MARIA.

SHIN'S A LITTLE WEIRD. DON'T MIND HIM.
Chatter
IT'S TOO BAD FOR YOU, THOUGH. ST. KATRIA'S UNIFORM IS SO MUCH CUTER.
Chatter
Stand
THE ST. KATRIA UNIFORM ALWAYS GETS VOTED THE CUTEST ONE IN KANAGAWA PREFECTURE.
TMP TMP
TOTSUKA IS ALWAYS AT THE BOTTOM OF THE LIST.
Ha ha ha
POLAR OPPO-SITES.
WHERE'RE YOU HEADED, SHIN?
I'M SKIP-PING.
YOUR CROSS NECKLACE IS ADORABLE, MARIA.
WHERE DID YOU BUY IT?
OH... ONE OF THE SISTERS GAVE IT TO ME.
CAN I SEE?
SO THERE ACTUALLY ARE "SISTERS"?
WOW.
REALLY?

CAN I TRY IT ON?
I'VE NEVER SEEN ONE LIKE THIS.
IT'S A PARTICULAR TYPE OF CROSS...
Maria's doing pretty well.
Yusuke, can I borrow your Power Pro game?
WOW, YOU SURE KNOW A LOT. ARE YOU RELIGIOUS?
DID YOU HAVE WORSHIP SERVICES AT ST. KATRIA?
twirl twirl
SO YOU ALL BELIEVE IN CHRIST THEN?!
THAT'S KINDA KOOKY.
...
WE DON'T HAVE ANYTHING LIKE THAT HERE.
Sorry!
OUR UNIFORMS AREN'T CUTE EITHER.
NO, IT'S NOT LIKE THAT.
POOR MARIA, YOU'VE REALLY FALLEN DOWN IN THE RANKS, HUH?
HEY, DO YOU THINK YOU'RE BETTER THAN US?
Like, St. Katria's was sooo special?

YOU'RE THE ONES TRYING TO LOOK DOWN ON ME.
Chirp
Chirp
DONG
DONG
BIRDS CAN FLY WHEREVER THEY WANT.
DONG
FLUTTER
YOU KNOW, GOD DOESN'T HAVE WINGS.

EVEN THE DEVIL HAS WINGS...

SHE'S PROBABLY UP THERE CRYING.
SHE CAME BACK TO AN EMPTY CLASS-ROOM...
...AND HER UNIFORM WAS IN SHREDS.
YOU TOOK HER UNIFORM APART FAST!
I'M GOOD WITH MY HANDS.
Ha ha ha ha ha
A flag!
Awe-some.
AREN'T YOU GIRLS SUPPOSED TO CLEAN UP TODAY?
Yeah.
WHOEVER MADE HER TAKE OUT THE TRASH, GOOD JOB!
MAKING IT INTO A FLAG WAS PURE GENIUS.
TH-THUMP

WE'RE DONE ALREADY.
YUSUKE, YOU SHOULD GO HOME.
WAIT! HAVE YOU SEEN SHIN?
NOPE.
I WONDER WHERE HE WENT...
See you, Yusuke.
Bye!
ON THE DAY I WAS EXPELLED...
...THE PERSON WHO I'D THOUGHT WAS MY BEST FRIEND SAID...
Amazing...

"YOU TAINT EVERYONE AROUND YOU."
THERE YOU ARE, SHIN.
YOU HAVEN'T BEEN IN CLASS SINCE RECESS.
I HATE BEING CALLED ON IN THE AFTERNOON.
BUT YOU'RE GOOD AT ENGLISH!
You even used to live abroad.
I DON'T LIKE SPEAKING IN PUBLIC.
MARIA GOT ON EVERYONE'S BAD SIDE...
WHO CARES?
THAT GIRL'S HOPELESS.
Amazing grace...
BELIEVING DOESN'T GUARANTEE YOU'LL BE SAVED.
EVER SINCE THAT MOMENT...

...I'VE JUST WANTED TO RUN AWAY.
How sweet the sound...
SHE HAS A BEAUTIFUL VOICE.
IS THAT IN ENGLISH?
...that saved a wretch...
SOME-ONE'S SINGING...
"HOW SWEET THE SOUND...

...like me...
I HATE MYSELF.
HUH? ARE THOSE THE LYRICS?
"...THAT SAVED A WRETCH LIKE ME"?
WHAT SONG IS IT?
I once was lost...
IT'S A CHRISTIAN HYMN.
I'M SORRY.

...but now I'm found.
Was blind, but now I see...
I WANT TO CHANGE.
OH! MARIA...
I WANT TO BE ABLE TO SAY "I LOVE YOU" TO SOMEONE.

I WANT TO BE ABLE TO SAY I LOVE MYSELF...
...AND MEAN IT FROM THE BOTTOM OF MY HEART.

OH.
SORRY, WE DIDN'T MEAN TO EAVES-DROP.
YOU SING REALLY WELL.
SORRY ABOUT EARLIER.

YOU CREATED AN OPPORTUNITY FOR ME TO TALK TO EVERYONE, BUT I BLEW IT.
WHEN YOU SAID MY UNIFORM DIDN'T LOOK GOOD.
YOU WERE BEING A JERK ON PURPOSE.
HUH? OPPOR-TUNITY?
IT...
IT WAS NOTHING!
IS THAT WHAT HAPPENED?
NO! I-
SO THAT'S HOW YOU REALLY ARE, HUH?
JUST STOP TALK-ING!
YOU WERE LOOKING OUT FOR ME.
I WASN'T!

YOU TWO SUIT EACH OTHER SO WELL.
DUM DUM DUM DU-MM
WHAT'S THAT SUPPOSED TO MEAN?
DON'T BE EMBAR-RASSED.
THE SCHOOL IS NOW CLOSED FOR THE DAY.
PLEASE LEAVE THE CAMPUS PROMPTLY.
DUM DUM DUM DUM DUM DUM
HEY...
I GUESS THEY CHANGED THE MUSIC FOR THE END OF THE DAY.
ISN'T THIS THE SONG YOU WERE JUST SINGING, MARIA?
THIS VERSION'S PRETTY CHEERFUL!

DUM DUM DUM DUM
THE P.A. MUSIC CHANGES EVERY MONTH.
THIS SOUNDS AND FEELS WAY DIFFERENT FROM YOUR SONG EARLIER.
IS IT REALLY A HYMN?
It's a different arrange-ment.
DUM DUM DUM DUM DUM DUM
DUM DUM
HEY, MARIA.
ARE YOU COMING TO SCHOOL TOMORROW?
DUM DUM DUM DUM DUM DUM

OF COURSE I AM.

OH, WAIT. I FORGOT.
YOU WANT TO SEE ME THAT BADLY? DON'T WORRY, I'LL BE HERE! ♡
Tilt
HA!
DROP DEAD!!
ZWAK
THIS "LOVELY SPIN" THING IS TRICKY.
SHOULD I HAVE ADDED, "I WANT TO SEE YOU TOO"?
Ha ha ha ha
THAT'S EVEN WORSE!

BUT IT DOESN'T MATTER IF IT'S TRUE OR NOT, RIGHT?
YOU LIAR.
MARIA IS...
MARIA KAWAI IS A DEVIL.
FWUP

DID SHE JUST SMILE...?
BUT I THINK...
...SHE'S A BEAUTIFUL ONE.

A Devil and Her Love Song

Song 2
A Devil and Her Love Song

HEY, THAT'S HER! MARIA KAWAI!
OH, THAT GIRL FROM ST. KATRIA?
SHE'S REALLY PRETTY...
tmp
tmp
SURE, I GUESS. BUT SOMEONE FROM CLASS C SAID...
tmp
...THAT WHEN SHE INTRODUCED HERSELF...
...SHE WAS BRAGGING ABOUT HOW SHE GOT EXPELLED FOR BEATING UP A TEACHER.
tmp
tmp

tmp
tmp
tmp
GOOD MORNING, MARIA!
NO SHOES TODAY? IS GOING BAREFOOT A NEW HEALTH FAD?
Beam
NOT EVERYTHING IS A JOKE, YUSUKE KANDA.
MUR-MUR
MUR-MUR
THIS WAS IN MY SHOES THIS MORNING.
...
A water balloon filled with ink
SQUIRT
When you step on it, it explodes!
I DIDN'T CHECK THEM FOR BOOBY TRAPS. SILLY ME.

I GUESS PEOPLE HERE DON'T LIKE ME VERY MUCH.
WHUP
YUSUKE, LISTEN TO THIS!
HUH? WHAT?
FWIP
NIPPACHI FREAKED OUT WHEN I SAID HER TESTS BLEW AWAY.
Hee hee
SHE'S SO GULLI-BLE.
ISN'T SHE FUNNY?

tmp
tmp
UGH, SHE'S SO STUCK-UP.
SHE DOESN'T EVEN TRY TO TALK TO US.
REALLY?
BUT WE'RE TALKING ABOUT SOMEONE SHE DOESN'T KNOW.
MAYBE SHE'S BEING CONSIDERATE AND TRYING NOT TO INTRUDE.
SHING
GRRRR!
WHOSE SIDE ARE YOU ON, YUSUKE?!
DON'T LET HER FOOL YOU!
YOU'RE TOO NICE!
WHAT?
OH...

RAGH
RAGH!!
"I DIDN'T WANT TO INTRUDE."
SO THAT'S HOW IT'S DONE...
"YOU'RE OBVIOUSLY TRYING TO EXCLUDE ME."
THAT'S WHAT I WOULD'VE SAID.
Just as well I didn't say anything.
SO THAT'S THE LOVELY SPIN, HUH?
And then you tilt your head like this.
CUTE BOY
tmp
tmp
I GUESS NEW FRIENDSHIPS START WHEN SOMEBODY CHOOSES YOU, NOT THE OTHER WAY AROUND.
IT'S MY SECOND DAY HERE.
SCRUB
SCRUB

AND NOBODY'S CHOSEN ME.
Shhk
FSSSSH
THWACK!
SPLASH
AGH!
WELL, IF IT ISN'T SHIN MEGURO.
IF YOU'RE GOING TO SKIP CLASS, YOU OUGHT TO CHOOSE A BETTER SPOT TO HIDE.
drip
drip
...
Shouldn't you be apolo-gizing...?
fizzle
And why do you know my name?
OH, YEAH. THE LOVELY SPIN...

TILT
IF YOU START SMOKING YOUNG, YOU'LL DIE YOUNG TOO. ♡
DON'T JINX ME!
Do you want me to die?!
SHIN MEGURO.
WHAT?
WHO'S NIPPACHI?
THAT DIDN'T GO SO WELL.
I HEARD PEOPLE TALKING ABOUT SOMEONE WITH THAT NAME.
NO CLUE. I DON'T KNOW EVERYONE IN CLASS.

WELL, THERE'S NO ONE IN CLASS C WHOSE NAME EVEN SOUNDS SIMILAR.
YOU MEMORIZED EVERYONE'S NAMES?
NIPPACHI, I FOUND ONE OF YOUR TESTS!
YOU ONLY GOT 5 PERCENT? SERIOUSLY?

WELL ...
YOU HAVE TO AT LEAST GET 28 PERCENT, NIPPACHI.
"NIPPA-CHI"?
HUH?
OH, MARIA...
HER NAME IS TOMOYO KOHSAKA. WHY CALL HER NIPPACHI?
SILENCE
...
SHUT UP. WHAT'S IT TO YOU?
UM... WELL...
I GRIN A LOT, AND THE KANJI CHARACTERS FOR "GRIN" SOUND LIKE THE ONES FOR "TWENTY-EIGHT." PUT "TWO" AND "EIGHT" TOGETHER, SO...
... "NIPPA-CHI."
Y-YEAH. IT'S 'CAUSE SHE ALWAYS SMILES LIKE THIS.

I SEE.
EXCEPT YOU THINK THEY'RE ALL IDIOTS, DON'T YOU, TOMOYO KOHSAKA?
WHAT —?
WHY WOULD ANYONE THINK WE'RE IDIOTS?
ESPECIALLY NIPPACHI?
IT'S THE OTHER WAY AROUND!
YOU'RE THE ONE WHO'S ACTING LIKE WE'RE STUPID!

YOU SUCK.
AND YOU REALLY PISS US OFF.
Un-believable!
C'mon, Nippa-chi.
THAT MARIA KAWAI'S A PIECE OF WORK.
SHE LOOKS DOWN HER NOSE AT EVERYONE.
SHE THINKS SHE'S SO SUPERIOR!
TOTALLY.
SHE HAS "ST. KATRIA" WRITTEN ALL OVER HER.
SO ANNOYING.

SHE ACTS LIKE SHE'S SO SPECIAL, EVEN THOUGH SHE GOT EXPELLED!
WE HAVE TO PUT HER IN HER PLACE.
YEAH, FOR HER OWN GOOD.
DON'T YOU THINK, NIPPACHI?
WELL...
HOW SHOULD I PUT THIS? YOU HAD SOME... ISSUES...AT YOUR OLD SCHOOL, RIGHT?
NOW, I DON'T WANT TO BE PREJU-DICED...
...BUT THERE'S BEEN AN ACCUSA-TION.

M-MARIA WAS BULLYING ME EARLIER.
SO THAT'S WHAT NIPPACHI HERE'S SAYING.
RIGHT?
Y-YES, SIR.
NIPPACHI SEEMS TO BE QUITE FRIGHTENED OF YOU.
NOW LET'S HEAR YOUR SIDE.

SHE'S NOT AFRAID AT ALL.
NOBODY MATTERS VERY MUCH TO TOMOYO KOHSAKA.
"KOHSAKA"? OH, YOU MEAN NIPPACHI.
WELL, AT ANY RATE, BULLYING ISN'T TOLERATED.
IF IT HAPPENS AGAIN, YOU'LL BE EXPELLED.
BUT THIS TIME, WRITE AN ESSAY REFLECTING ON THIS EXPERIENCE.
UPON REFLECTION
NAME
WELL? WHAT THEN?
TELL US WHAT HAPPENED NEXT, NIPPACHI!

RAGH RAGH
A PERSONAL ESSAY? IS THAT ALL?
SHHK
YOU SHOULD'VE PLAYED IT UP MORE, NIPPACHI. ACT MORE LIKE A VICTIM.
THE GIRLS ARE ALL RILED UP. What happened?
YUSUKE.
YEAH?
WHY WOULD SOMEONE LEARN THE NAMES OF EVERYONE IN CLASS?
THAT'S OBVIOUS!
SO THAT YOU CAN BE FRIENDS WITH EVERYONE!
REALLY?

A WELCOME PARTY?
UH-HUH. UM...
WE ALL HOPE YOU'LL COME.
UPON REFLECTION
NAME
CLASS
I WANT TO PATCH THINGS UP TOO.
THERE'S NO NEED. IT'S NOT LIKE WE'RE FRIENDS.
OH...
O-OKAY...
I guess?
twitch
SHE WANTS TO BE FRIENDS WITH EVERYONE...?

I DIDN'T MEAN THAT JUST NOW. I'M SORRY.
I'LL GO.
OH ...
HA HA...
SHFF
ALL RIGHT, THEN!
LET'S HEAD OUT-SIDE.
WE'RE GOING TO KARA-OKE.
EVERY-ONE ELSE WENT AHEAD, SO—
TOMOYO KOHSAKA.
HUH?
MAYBE FRIEND-SHIP...
...CAN'T BEGIN UNTIL SOMEONE CHOOSES YOU.

BUT...
...THAT DOESN'T MEAN YOU DON'T GET TO MAKE A CHOICE TOO.
YOU CAN'T DO THAT...
...UNLESS YOU KNOW WHO THEY ARE.
AND THEY CAN'T CHOOSE YOU...
...UNTIL THEY KNOW WHO *YOU* ARE.

SO...
...IT'S BEST THAT I GO. EVEN IF EVERYONE ENDS UP SEEING...
...HOW ROTTEN WE REALLY ARE...
TOMOYO KOHSAKA?

SHOVE
AH...

THERE'S NOTHING ROTTEN ABOUT ME!
I'M NOT LIKE YOU!!
TO-MO...
TWINGE
NGH...

SO STUPID...
I KNOW THIS "WELCOME PARTY" OF THEIRS...
...IS JUST ANOTHER PLAN TO HARASS ME.
IT'S NEVER EASY...
...TO DEAL WITH SO MUCH HATE.
AT LEAST IT'S NOT BROKEN.
ZZZT

BUT I KNOW WHAT THE SISTERS WOULD SAY.
"DOUBTING PEOPLE RIGHT FROM THE OUTSET IS FOOLISH."
THROB
"YOU NEVER KNOW WHEN A TRUE FRIEND IS WAITING FOR YOU."
THOSE WHO BELIEVE WILL BE SAVED.
SHIN MEGU-RO.
WHERE DO PEOPLE GO FOR KARAOKE AROUND HERE?
TCH
KARA-OKE?! WHY?

I'M MEETING PEOPLE THERE, BUT I FORGOT TO ASK WHAT THE PLACE IS CALLED.
...
HOW SHOULD I KNOW?
I've never gone.
IT'S PROBABLY NEAR YOKOHAMA STATION.
I SEE.
THAT MAKES SENSE. YOU DON'T SEEM LIKE YOU'D ENJOY SINGING IN FRONT OF PEOPLE.
I BET YOU SING BY YOURSELF IN THE SHOWER AND THEN DENY IT IF ANYONE HEARS YOU.
Bull's-eye
You...!
SORRY.
fwip
BUT...
WHO ARE YOU MEETING?

...I NEED TO KNOW FOR SURE.
WILL HAVING FAITH SAVE ME?
OH, YOU KNOW. EVERYONE.
STRIDE
TMP
TMP

WHAT...?
IF IT'S ACTUALLY TRUE...
HEY, SHIN!
WHERE'VE YOU BEEN?
Let's go.
CAN I SLEEP OVER TONIGHT?
EVERY-ONE...?!
?
...I MIGHT EVEN BE ABLE...
...TO TRANSFORM MYSELF.

A Devil and Her Love Song

Song 3
A Devil and Her Love Song

Aoyama Office
Karaoke
Manga Capsule
Karaoke
EVERYONE IN THE WORLD LOVES THEMSELVES BEST.
SHUP
THAT'S TRUE EVEN WHEN YOU FALL IN LOVE WITH SOMEBODY.
BEING WITH THAT PERSON MAKES YOU MORE IN LOVE WITH YOURSELF.
¥2000 PER HOUR
ARE THERE ANY TOTSUKA STUDENTS HERE?
UM... NOT RIGHT NOW.
DID YOU SEE HER?
SHE'S GORGEOUS.
THINK SHE'S A MODEL?
BUT BEING AROUND MARIA KAWAI...

...MAKES ME LOATHE MYSELF.
OW...
MARIA'S GETTING TOGETHER WITH THE WHOLE CLASS?
MEW!
NO ONE INVITED ME!
...
I WAS LEFT OUT?!
MAYBE THEY'RE SHUN-NING YOU.
ZWAK
THAT'S SO MEAN!
BUT I'M DOING MY VERY BEST TO BE LOVELY!
WHY WOULD THEY SHUN ME?!

IF YOU'RE EVERYBODY'S FRIEND, YOU'RE ALSO NOBODY'S FRIEND, MR. POPULARITY.
WHAT'S WITH YOU, SHIN?
HEY, WAIT UP!
You're acting scary.
I'M LEAVING.
AND YOU'RE NOT COMING.
BANG
BUT ...! SHIN ...!

trudge
trudge
THAT WAS CRUEL.
I REALLY DON'T FEEL LIKE GOING HOME TODAY...
UNH...
SOB...
SOB...
SNFF...
...
I THINK MARIA IS BASICALLY LIKE A MIRROR.
FWUFF
WHAT'S WRONG?
ARE YOU OKAY?
SHE MAKES YOU SEE EVERY SINGLE FLAW IN YOURSELF. IT'S EXHAUSTING.

THERE'S SOMETHING DEMONIC ABOUT HOW SHE BRINGS OUT THE WORST IN YOU.
ARE THERE ANY TOTSUKA STUDENTS HERE RIGHT NOW?
TOTSUKA? LET ME SEE...
HERE'S OUR WAIT LIST.
YOU CAN TAKE A LOOK.
If you'd like to be on the wait list, please write your name clearly.
2 Hanada♥
5 Totsuka High, 1-C
Asai

HEY, MARIA! IT'S ABOUT TIME!
WE'VE BEEN WAITING!
COME SIT DOWN!
RIGHT HERE IN THE MIDDLE, GUEST OF HONOR!
AFTER ALL, IT'S YOUR WELCOME PARTY!
WHERE IS SHE, ANYWAY?
CHAK
SORRY I'M LATE.
NAH, IT'S FINE.
I BET IT WAS NIPPA-CHI'S FAULT.
TOMOYO KOHSAKA? SHE LOST IT.

WHAT ...?
UM... I DON'T GET WHAT YOU MEAN.
SHE LOST IT AND RAN OFF SOME- WHERE.
SO I CAME BY MYSELF.
IS THAT A PROBLEM? DOES SHE HAVE TO BE HERE?
HUH?
N-NO, IT'S TOTALLY FINE.
RIGHT?
YEAH, SURE.

UGH, NIPPACHI'S SO USELESS!
I CAN'T BELIEVE SHE BAILED ON US.
NOW WHAT DO WE DO?
YEAH, IF NIPPACHI'S NOT HERE, WE CAN'T EXACTLY GET HER WASTED AND BLAME IT ON MARIA.
I EVEN SNUCK IN ALL THAT BEER.
WELL, YOU PLAY THE VICTIM THEN!
GET HER IN TROUBLE.
NO WAY! WHY ME?
BECAUSE SOMEBODY HAS TO MAKE MARIA LOOK LIKE A DEVIL CHILD.
JUST PRE-TEND.
PRETEND YOU'RE BEING BULLIED!
PRE...

IF I PLAY THE VICTIM ONCE, I'LL ALWAYS HAVE TO DO IT!
FORGET IT!
WHAT THE HECK IS WRONG WITH YOU?
WHAT?
CUT IT OUT.
FIGHTING WITH EACH OTHER IS POINTLESS.
LET'S COME UP WITH A NEW PLAN.
THEN YOU THINK OF SOMETHING!
UM... HOW ABOUT THIS?
WE'LL ORDER TONS OF FOOD AND LEAVE MARIA WITH THE BILL.
THAT'LL WORK!

WE'LL KILL HER WITH KINDNESS...
...AND THEN DITCH HER AT THE LAST MINUTE!
Ta-dah
NEXT, WE WANT...
...SOME FRUIT AND SEVEN CHOCOLATE PARFAITS.
ACTUALLY, YOU KNOW WHAT? JUST BRING US EVERYTHING ON PAGE THREE.
MARIIIAAA, WHICH ONE DO YOU WANT? YOU PICK FIRST!
IT'S ALL DELICIOUS, MARIA.
Eat up!
Haha
OKAY, HOW ABOUT A SONG?
SING FOR US, MARIA!
Haha

I'D RATHER LISTEN.
AW, DON'T BE LIKE THAT! I WANT TO HEAR YOU SING.
DON'T FORCE HER.
SOME PEOPLE JUST LIKE LISTENING. RIGHT, MARIA?
OH, OKAY. SORRY, MARIA.
IT'S FINE.
WHAT IF WE ALL SING?
HOW ABOUT THAT?
WE WANT YOU TO HAVE FUN.
IT'S YOUR PARTY, AFTER ALL!
YOU'RE RIGHT.
I'M SORRY.
YAY! WHAT DO YOU WANT TO SING? SOMETHING NEW?
WHO DO YOU LISTEN TO?

SERI-OUSLY?
YOU DON'T KNOW ANY SONGS ...?
DON'T YOU LISTEN TO MUSIC?
WELL, WHAT CAN YOU SING?
OLDIES? ANIME STUFF?
CHURCH HYMNS.
KIDS' FOLK SONGS. THE KIND IN TEXT-BOOKS.
Conser-vative
PFFFT
NO WAY!
YOU'RE A CATHOLIC SCHOOL-GIRL, ALL RIGHT!
Ahhahahaha

WSP
PATHETIC.
FWP
OKAY, LET'S PICK SOMETHING EVEN MARIA CAN SING.
WHAT'S A GOOD KIDS' SONG?
Sorry. I DON'T KNOW ANY OF THOSE.
Ha ha ha ha ha!
WHATEVER.
JUST PICK SOMETHING.
FLASH
CHILDHOOD FAVORITE
"UNDER THE BIG CHESTNUT TREE"
MARIA, YOU CAN SING THIS, RIGHT?
I MEAN, IT'S YOUR PARTY 'N' ALL.
THE GUEST OF HONOR HAS TO SING!
INTRO
OKAY, IT'S STARTING.

YOU CAN DO IT, MARIA!
GO FOR IT!
I NEED TO KNOW FOR SURE.
WILL HAVING FAITH SAVE ME?
...WILL IT ALL BE OVER?
Shup
AND...
...IF I STOP BELIEVING...
UNDER...

OH, I'M SORRY!
I ACCIDENTALLY TURNED IT OFF.
I WILL BELIEVE.
Sorry, Maria.
DANGLE
I WILL BELIEVE!
Under...
...the big...
...chestnut tree.

You and me...
Let's play together...
...under the big chestnut tree.
IT'S SCARY...
...BUT I HAVE TO DO IT.

We'll all talk together...
...in a big circle...
I HAVE TO DO IT UNTIL THE END.
...under the—
STOP IT!

URK...
DON'T TELL ME YOU'RE SINGING SERIOUSLY?
HA HA...
THAT'S STUPID!
ARE YOU FOR REAL?
OF COURSE I'M SERIOUS.
WHAT?
IF I WEREN'T SERIOUS...
...I WOULDN'T BE HERE AT ALL.
AND IF YOU WEREN'T SERIOUS...
...YOU WOULDN'T HAVE PLANNED THIS PARTY FOR ME.

SO WHY IN THE WORLD WOULDN'T I TAKE THIS SERIOUSLY?
YOU'RE NOT TOO BRIGHT FOR A ST. KATRIA GIRL.
LISTEN, MARIA.
DON'T GET THE WRONG IDEA.
NONE OF US GIVE A CRAP ABOUT YOU.
YOU GET ON OUR NERVES, OKAY?

WE DON'T CARE AT ALL!
THIS "PARTY" WAS A JOKE!
EVERYONE HATES YOU!
OR THEY'D HATE YOU IF THEY KNEW YOU EXISTED!
YOU'RE NOTHING SPECIAL.
YOU'RE JUST IRRITATING.
YOU REALLY BUG ME!
DIE, FOR ALL I CARE!
SAY SOMETHING, YOU GUYS!
...
HMM. IS THAT YOUR TAKE ON A LOVELY SPIN?
EXCUSE ME?
YOU'RE SAYING YOU CAN'T STOP THINKING ABOUT ME.
THAT'S ALL I'M HEARING.
WHAT'RE YOU TALKING ABOUT?!

I SAID THE EXACT OPPOSITE!
PAY ATTENTION!
THIS IS IT.
KRI...
WE'RE HERE!
IF YOU DIDN'T CARE, YOU WOULDN'T HAVE BOTHERED THROWING ME A PARTY.
WHAT?!
flinch
DO YOU SERIOUSLY STILL THINK WE WANT YOU HERE?
I have faith in you. ♡
TILT
GAH!!
ARE...
ARE YOU THREATENING US?
Eeeek!
UM...
DOES SHE THINK THAT'S LOVELY?
HUH?

OF COURSE I'M NOT.
LIAR!!
YOU'RE PLANNING TO GET BACK AT US!
Why would I do that, silly? ♡
Tilt
IT'S TOTALLY OBVIOUS!
HMM. THE LOVELY SPIN'S BACK-FIRING...
I CAN BELIEVE ABSOLUTELY ANYTHING I WANT. ♡
GOT A PROBLEM WITH THAT?
OH, WHATEVER! HAVE IT YOUR WAY!
THAT'LL JUST MAKE IT MORE FUN...
...WHEN YOU FINALLY NOTICE WE'RE JERKING YOU AROUND!

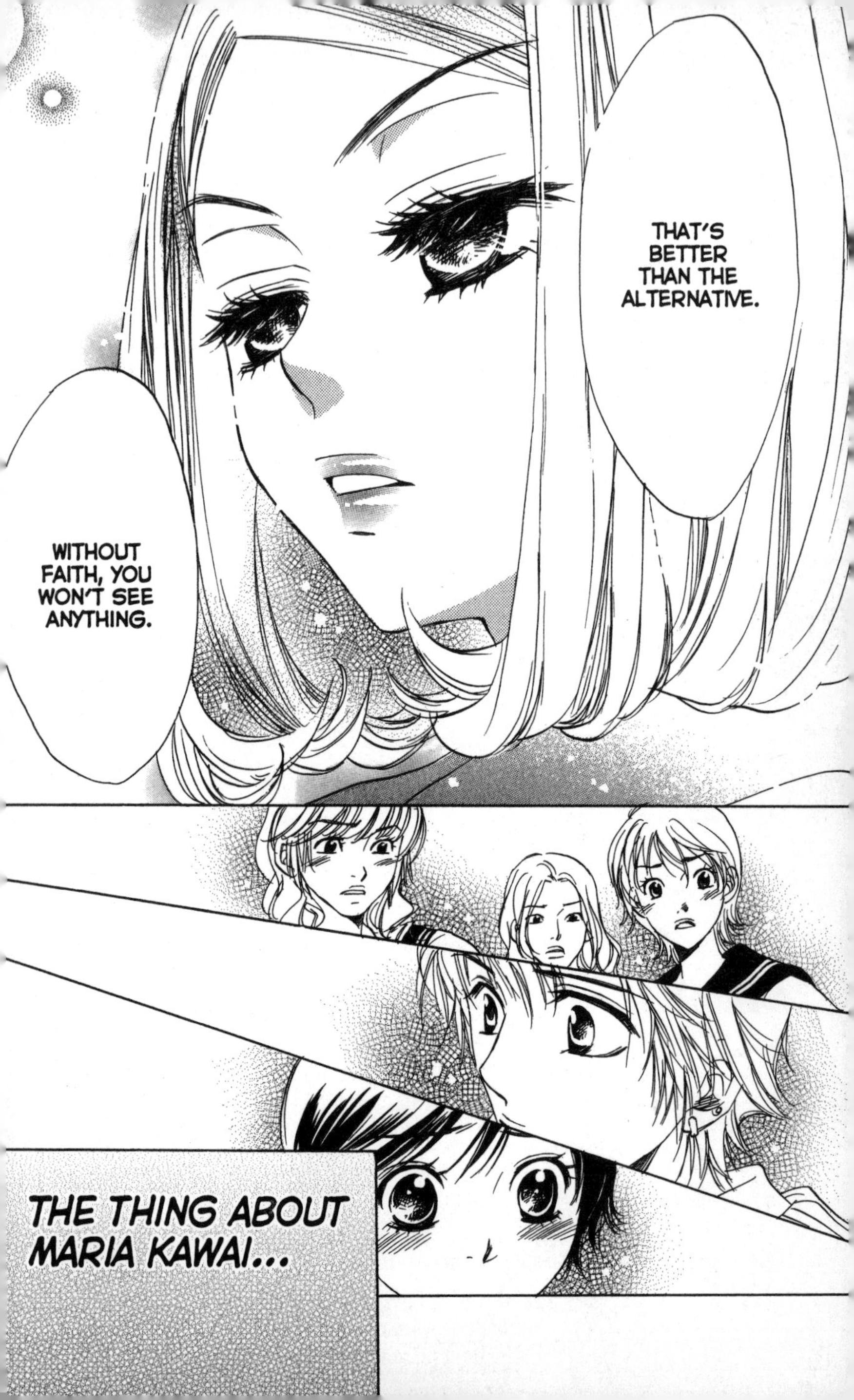
THAT'S BETTER THAN THE ALTERNATIVE.
WITHOUT FAITH, YOU WON'T SEE ANYTHING.
THE THING ABOUT MARIA KAWAI...

...IS THAT SHE MAKES YOU FACE...
MANGA CAPSULE
KARA-OKE
KARA-OKE
...ALL THE SAD THINGS YOU NEVER WANTED TO SEE AGAIN.
SHE FORCES YOU TO STARE AT THEM. SHE'S LIKE THE DEVIL INCARNATE.

A Devil and
Her Love Song

A Devil and Her Love Song
Song 4

YOU HEARD ME! A TALL, PRETTY GIRL WHO'S A HUGE SNOB!
IS SHE HERE OR NOT?
How many times do I have to...
HUFF HUFF HUFF HUFF HUFF...
MAYBE YOU SHOULD SIT DOWN.
...
...ask ...?
KARAOKE
G
AAARGH!
DO I HAVE TO CHECK EVERY SINGLE KARAOKE JOINT AROUND YOKOHAMA STATION...?

WHY AM I LOOKING FOR HER, ANYHOW?!
I SHOULD LEAVE HER ALONE!
Oh
...
SKRCH
UGH!
SO ANNOYING...
THIS IS NO GOOD, MARIA!
YOU CAN'T ABANDON A FRIEND JUST 'CAUSE SHE'S A PAIN TO DEAL WITH.
Karaoke
2F
2F
5F

YOU KNOCKED HER DOWN AND RAN OFF?
I FOUND HER CRYING IN THE HALLWAY...
SHE'S WONDERING WHY YOU HATE HER SO MUCH.
Y-YUSUKE ...?!
WHAT'RE YOU DOING HERE ...?
SORRY FOR DROPPING BY!
I KNOW I WASN'T INVITED, BUT I DIDN'T WANT TO MISS THE WELCOME PARTY.
FWUFF
I SAW NIPPACHI ON MY WAY HOME.
SHE LOOKED SO UNHAPPY...
...SO I TOLD HER WE SHOULD FIND MARIA AND CLEAR THE AIR.

YOU DON'T ACTUALLY HATE HER, DO YOU, MARIA?
MAYBE YOU SHOULD APOLOGIZE.
AH... HA HA...
I'M SORRY.
FORTY-EIGHT THOUSAND YEN*?!
WHY'D YOU ORDER SO MUCH?!
*About $625

OKAY, THAT'S 5,000 YEN* EACH.
I'LL PAY THE DIFFERENCE.
TOO BAD WE'RE LEAVING. I JUST GOT HERE!
I didn't get to sing.
*About $65
WELL, WE'RE HEADING OUT.
LET'S WALK TO THE STATION TOGETHER!
WE'VE... GOT TO STOP SOMEWHERE.
LET'S GO, NIPPA-CHI.
HA HA...
Tilt
See you all tomorrow. ♡
Brrr
Why'd you bring Yusuke?
Nippa-chi, I swear—!
SHOVE

YUSUKE KANDA.
THE TRUTH IS, I DON'T HATE TOMOYO KOHSAKA.
OH? THAT'S GOOD.
BUT...
...SHE'S NOT SOMEONE I'D PICK AS A FRIEND.
BUT MAYBE IF YOU GET TO KNOW HER–
TILT
YUSUKE KANDA.
YEAH?
WHAT CAN I DO...
...TO FIT IN BETTER WITH OTHER PEOPLE?

STARE
TURN
...I DON'T REALLY KNOW, MARIA.
LET'S HEAD OVER TO THE STATION.
IF I BELIEVE, MAYBE I'LL BE SAVED...
...BUT WHO KNOWS? IT MIGHT NOT HAPPEN IMMEDIATELY.
NO, YOU GO AHEAD.
I WANT TO TAKE MY TIME.

MAYBE THINGS WON'T CHANGE TODAY, OR EVEN TOMORROW.
HUFF
HUFF
GOOD THINGS DON'T HAPPEN RIGHT AWAY...
...BECAUSE I DON'T DESERVE THEM, RIGHT?
THROB
THROB
THROB
BUT I'M STARTING TO THINK MAYBE I'M JUST NOT NOTICING THEM.
limp

IF I DON'T BELIEVE GOOD THINGS WILL HAPPEN...
...WHY WOULD I LOOK FOR THEM?
Totsuka High School
GLANCE
I THINK...
Totsuka
limp
...THAT I'LL NEVER FIND THEM IF I DON'T HAVE FAITH.
Shhk

IF I DON'T BELIEVE IN MYSELF, THEN...
THERE YOU ARE, MARIA!
RIGHT, YUSUKE-? OH, ISN'T HE HERE YET?
Geez!
LOOK AT NIPPACHI'S FOOT!
YUSUKE SAID YOU PUSHED HER YESTERDAY.

NIPPACHI DIDN'T RAT YOU OUT, BUT IT'S YOUR FAULT, ISN'T IT?
YOU'RE TERRIBLE!
WELL, SHE'S VIOLENT ENOUGH TO GET EXPELLED FROM ST. KATRIA.
PEOPLE NEVER CHANGE.
SCARY, HUH?
Mor-ning!
HOW'RE YOU GONNA MAKE IT UP TO HER?
OH NO! WHAT HAPPENED TO YOUR LEG?
IS THAT FROM YESTER-DAY?
O-OH...
HA HA.

YOU'D BETTER SIT DOWN AND REST IT!
THAT'S NOT GOOD ENOUGH!
I'LL DO YOUR SHARE OF CLEANING UP.
YOU'RE TOO LAID BACK, YUSUKE.
What would you call good enough?
HUH?
MARIA OUGHT TO DO IT!
SHE SHOULD TIDY UP EVERY MORNING IN NIPPACHI'S PLACE!
SHE SHOULD TAKE OVER ALL OF NIPPACHI'S RESPONSIBILITIES.
Ha ha ha
Girls are scary!
SHE SHOULD STRAIGHT OUT **BE** HER!

NO.
HUH?!
LOOK, YOU–
I'LL DO WHATEVER I CAN TO HELP.
I'LL CLEAN, CARRY HER THINGS, WALK TO CLASS WITH HER...
BUT I CAN'T BE TOMOYO KOHSAKA.
I CAN'T DO THINGS I DISLIKE AND SMILE AS IF I LOVE IT.

THE ONLY PERSON I CAN BE IS ME.
WHAT ...?

GRAB
WHO DO YOU THINK YOU ARE...?!
SLIP
OW!
CRASH
EEE!
LOOK AT HER!
LIKE THEY SAY...
Ha!
...PRIDE GOES BEFORE A FALL!
FWEE!
HEY...!

MARIA, ARE YOU OKAY?!
WHAT'S WITH YOU, YUSUKE?
IT'S HER OWN FAULT! SHE DOESN'T EVEN FEEL BAD.
I can't see, Yusuke.
Move!
THAT'S GOING TOO FAR, GUYS!
NIPPACHI'S THE INJURED PARTY HERE.
Sor-ry.
MARIA, DID YOU REALLY PUSH HER DOWN?
I DIDN'T WANT TO SAY ANYTHING YESTER-DAY...
...BUT TO BE HONEST, IT DIDN'T SOUND RIGHT.
!
WHY ASK THAT NOW?
BE-CAUSE—

THERE'S NOTHING WORSE THAN FINDING OUT SOMEONE DIDN'T BELIEVE YOU...
...AFTER THE FACT.
THAT'S RIGHT.
HUH?
NIPPACHI, WHAT ABOUT YOUR CRUTCHES?
THIS IS EXACTLY LIKE WHAT HAPPENED THE DAY I GOT EXPELLED.
!
ARE YOU EVEN HURT?!
"YOU TAINT EVERYONE AROUND YOU.

"THE TRUTH IS, I'VE ALWAYS THOUGHT THAT."
I-I FELL DOWN THE STAIRS THIS MORNING...
ARE YOU KIDDING?
YOU'RE PUTTING WEIGHT ON IT!
UNBELIEV-ABLE!
SO YOU WERE LYING ABOUT HER PUSHING YOU DOWN TOO?
YOU'RE SUCH A LIAR.
MAYBE MARIA'S IN ON IT. SHE DIDN'T DENY IT.
WHAT ARE YOU TWO UP TO?
MARIA'S A LIAR TOO!
LIAR!
AND OF COURSE I KNEW...
LIAR!
...THAT WAS WHAT THEY THOUGHT OF ME.
LIAR!

THAT'S WHY GOD WOULD NEVER GIVE ME SOMETHING GOOD.
WHAT'S GOING ON IN HERE?
ZWAK
MARIA'S MAKING TROUBLE, SIR.
YOU AGAIN, MARIA?
WHEN YOU FALL FROM GRACE ONCE, YOU'RE A SCREW-UP FOREVER.
STILL...
I MADE A DECISION.

I'M GOING TO BELIEVE IN MYSELF.
BUT...
HANG ON, SIR!
THAT'S TOO—
BUT I...
TOSS
DON'T JUST STAND THERE, IDIOT.
WHERE'S THAT ACID TONGUE WHEN YOU REALLY NEED IT?
TCH!

SCOOP
OOF!
AND STOP STANDING ON THAT INJURED FOOT OF YOURS.
YOU KNOW...
...YOU'RE HEAVIER THAN YOU LOOK.

LET...
...LET ME...
...
STOP WRIG-GLING!
I'M TAKING YOU TO THE CLINIC AT THE STATION.
YU-SUKE!
TELL THE TEACHER SHE'S LEAVING EARLY...
...AND I'M CUTTING CLASS.
SLAM
BUT I'M RIGHT HERE...
SILENCE
MUR-MUR
WHAT WAS THAT...?
I'VE NEVER SEEN SHIN LIKE THAT.
I THOUGHT HE DIDN'T LIKE ATTENTION.
I'M KINDA SHOCKED...

ME TOO...
GAH!
Huff
I'M... NOT...
Huff
Huff
...THE ATHLETIC TYPE...
...
HUFF ...
OUT OF SHAPE
HUFF ...
SHOOT.
I DON'T UNDER-STAND...
Huff
Huff
Huff
...WHAT'S GOING ON. NOT AT ALL.

IT HAPPENED SO SUDDENLY...
Amazing grace...
How sweet the sound...
...AND I WAS SO HAPPY AND SCARED...
...THAT I COULDN'T FIND THE WORDS TO EXPLAIN IT.
...that saved a wretch like me...

A Devil and Her Love Song

A Devil and
Her Love Song
Song 5

I SHOULD'VE STAYED OUT OF IT.
I once was lost...
SOME PEOPLE JUST DON'T GET ALONG WITH PEOPLE.
横浜駅西口
...but now I'm found.
Was blind, but now...
I SHOULD'VE LEFT IT ALONE. IT'S NOT LIKE I CAN CHANGE ANYTHING.

SO WHY DO I KEEP GETTING INVOLVED WHEN IT'S HER?
...I see...
CRAP!
FREEZE
...
UH...
AWKWARD SILENCE
PEOPLE ARE STARING 'CAUSE YOU'RE SINGING.

OH...
I DIDN'T MEAN TO BOTHER YOU.
WELL, I DON'T THINK IT'S WHAT I'M DOING THAT'S FRUSTRATING ME.
I DIDN'T MEAN YOU HAD TO STOP.
I MEAN...
ER...
YOUR SING-ING...
...ISN'T BAD OR ANY-THING.
IT'S HER.

SORRY ABOUT THAT.
IT'S BECAUSE OF THIS WEIRD DISTANCE I FEEL BETWEEN ME AND MARIA KAWAI.

AOI CLINIC
YOU DON'T HAVE YOUR INSURANCE CARD?
THEN YOU'LL HAVE TO PAY UP FRONT AND GET REIM-BURSED.
THE CONSULTATION AND COLD PACK COME TO...
...
Empty-handed
I'LL COVER IT.
CAN I PAY WITH MY CELL?
FLIP
Credit at your age ...?
SORRY ...
SO...
...HOW'S YOUR FOOT FEELING?
AH.
IT'S NOTHING SERIOUS.

HEY, HOLD ON! ARE YOU SUPPOSED TO WALK ON IT?
GRAB
WHA
P
OH...
UM...
THE DOCTOR BANDAGED IT, SO I CAN WALK.
IT'S A STRAINED LIGAMENT. IT'S A BIT INFLAMED.
BUT I'LL BE FINE IN A COUPLE WEEKS IF I TAKE IT EASY.

SORRY FOR ALL THE TROUBLE.
WANT TO GO BUY SOME SHOES?
CLINIC SLIPPERS AREN'T THE BEST FOR WALKING OUTSIDE.
HERE, LET ME TAKE THAT—
TWITCH
HAVE IT YOUR WAY.
GO BACK TO SCHOOL OR WHAT-EVER.
FWIP
FINE.
WAIT!

I...
WHAT?
...REALLY AM SORRY.
...
WHAT'S WRONG WITH YOU?
WHY ARE YOU ACTING SO NERVOUS?
THAT'S WHAT'S GETTING ON MY NERVES.
ARE YOU MAD AT ME FOR DRAGGING YOU OUT OF SCHOOL?
NO.

THAT'S NOT IT.
THIS IS DIFFICULT FOR ME.
I DON'T KNOW.
I JUST KEEP APOLOGIZING.
I'M SCARED. I WANT TO RUN AWAY. BUT...I WANT TO HOLD ON TO HIM TOO.
IT'S ALMOST LIKE...
YOU'RE TALL, AND YOU DON'T SLOUCH.
THAT'S WHY PEOPLE THINK YOU'RE LOOKING DOWN ON THEM.

SHOES ARE THE FIRST PRIORITY!
YOU NEED TO BE ABLE TO WALK AROUND PROPERLY.
YOU'RE LOOKING ALL DEJECTED. THAT'S NOT YOU!
MART
FIND A GOOD, COMFORT-ABLE PAIR.
AND REMEMBER NOT TO GET YOUR USUAL SIZE.
I'M GONNA LOOK FOR A PAIR FOR MYSELF.

GO UP A SIZE—
SHING
ARE YOU KIDDING ME?
YOU'LL LOOK LIKE AN IDIOT IN THOSE FRILLY THINGS!
I BEG YOUR PARDON?
THE AESTHETIC IS GORGEOUS WITH THE BOWS AND SEQUINS!
FIERCE
AND LOOK AT THE STITCHING ON THE HEELS! THOSE WINGS ARE POSITIVELY ANGELIC!
UM... SORRY...
YEAH... ME TOO.
IT'S JUST...

...YOU SHOULD GET FLATS.
YOUR ANKLE'S TWISTED, AFTER ALL.
THAT'S TRUE.
ALL RIGHT.
Basic
Black ballet flats- ¥1,000!!
YES.
THESE FIT DECENTLY, AND THEY'RE GOOD FOR WALKING.
KEEP 'EM ON, AND I'LL GO PAY.
I'M GETTING SOME-THING TOO.
BCA MART
BCA MART
Aoi Clinic
Aoi Clinic

DID YOU BUY SHOES FOR YOURSELF SO I WOULDN'T FEEL BAD?
I...
I SAW A PAIR I WANTED, THAT'S ALL.
SOR—
STOP APOLOGIZING.
SHIN MEGURO.
DO YOU WANT TO HAVE LUNCH?
THERE'S A CHINESE BUN CART AT A PARK NEAR HERE.

WILL YOU GO WITH ME?
YOUR CELL PHONE?
NO CAN DO. CASH ONLY.
OH, NEVER MIND. TAKE THEM.
I'LL PUT IT ON YOUR TAB. PAY ME TOMOR-ROW!
THAT'S STINGY! YOU'RE TRYING TO MAKE US BUY MORE.
H-HEY ...
SO WHAT IF I AM? IF YOU DON'T LIKE IT, GIVE THOSE BACK.
NO, IT'S FINE.
...
CHINESE BUNS

DO YOU GO THERE A LOT?
SOMETIMES I WENT AFTER SCHOOL WHEN I WAS AT ST. KATRIA.
CRINKLE
SO YOU HAD FRIENDS TO HANG OUT WITH THEN?
NO, I WENT ALONE.
SORRY.
DON'T BE RIDICULOUS. WHY SHOULD YOU APOLOGIZE?
WANT ONE?
SURE.
CHOMP
?

THIS IS GROSS!
IT'S GOT A SPECIAL SYRUP FILLING.
IF IT'S NOT SWEET ENOUGH, ADD SOME HONEY.
HOW CAN YOU EAT THAT?!
GOOD, ISN'T IT?
SURE, IF YOU LIKE TORTURE!
Take it back.
UGH, I HATE SWEET STUFF!
IT DID OCCUR TO ME...
I HAD A FEELING YOU'D BE LIKE THAT.
"Chinese bun," she says!
GLUG
GLUG

BUT I REALLY LIKE THEM...
...SO I WANTED YOU TO TRY ONE.
THAT WAS SELFISH OF ME.
SWIPE
CRAM
YOU DON'T HAVE TO—
DON'T START!
I FELT LIKE EATING IT.
IT'S A FREE COUNTRY!

I'M SORRY—
DON'T START WITH THAT, EITHER!
BACK AT ST. KATRIA...
...THERE WAS A CHAPEL.

WE ALL CALLED IT THE PENANCE ROOM.
WE WERE SUPPOSED TO GO CONFESS OUR SINS TO GOD AND REFLECT ON THEM.
WHEN SOMETHING WAS REALLY WEIGHING ON THEM...
...MY CLASSMATES WENT THERE TO UNBURDEN THEMSELVES.
STUFF LIKE, "I DIDN'T STUDY," "I MADE MY FRIEND CRY," OR "I WENT ON A DATE EVEN THOUGH I HAVE A BOYFRIEND."
THE SISTERS LISTENED TO THEIR CONFESSIONS...
...AND PRETENDED TO BE SO KIND.
YOU KNOW, LIKE IN DETECTIVE SHOWS.
LIKE WHEN A COP IS NICE TO A SUSPECT...
...AND BUYS HIM DINNER AND TALKS ABOUT HIS FAMILY.
Um, what?

I COULDN'T STAND THE HYPOCRISY.
I NEVER WENT TO CONFESSION THERE. NOT ONCE.
BUT...
WHY AM I TELLING HIM ALL THIS?
IT'S LIKE...
...I'M ONE OF THEM—POURING MY HEART OUT AND EXPECTING FORGIVE-NESS.
WHAT'S THE BIG DEAL?
WHO CARES IF YOU CONFESS TO GOD OR A SISTER OR WHAT-EVER?
IT'S POINT-LESS.
I...

WHAT I DON'T LIKE...
...IS PEOPLE APOLOGIZING TO ME!
SQUEAK
YOU'RE RIGHT.
YOU'RE NOT GOD, AND YOU'RE CERTAINLY NOT A NUN.
I SUPPOSE I WANT HIM TO FORGIVE ME.
HE HAS SUCH A KIND STREAK...

BUT YOU'RE RIGHT HERE BESIDE ME, UNLIKE GOD.
THE IDEA OF YOU REJECTING ME IS MUCH MORE FRIGHTENING.
I DON'T WANT TO DO THINGS THAT ANNOY YOU.
THE BUNS WERE CERTAINLY A FLOP.
I'LL STOP APOLOGIZING TO YOU.

THESE ARE FOR YOU. TO PAY YOU BACK FOR THE BUNS!
I THOUGHT YOU SAID YOU BOUGHT SHOES FOR YOURSELF...

I REALLY SHOULD'VE LEFT HER ALONE.
DON'T YOU DARE APOLOGIZE.
THIS REALLY SUCKS. WHY THE HECK...

THEN... THANK YOU.
...DID I FALL FOR A DEVIL LIKE HER?
SHE'S REALLY A PIECE OF WORK.

SHE CAN PRETTY MUCH READ MY MIND.
THESE THINGS ARE HIDEOUS.
THE FRILLS-TO-UGLY RATIO IS REALLY HIGH.
OH, A STATISTIC.
OR ANALOGY?
You actually mean that, don't you...?
THERE'S ABSOLUTELY NO WAY I'LL EVER LET HER SEE...
...HOW I'M FEELING ABOUT HER.
OH...
MY FOOT'S TOO SWOLLEN FOR IT.
YOU KARATE-CHOPPED MY HEAD!
I'D NEVER BE ABLE TO STAND IT.

A Devil and
Her Love Song

MENU
A Devil and Her Love Song
Song 6

BLEEP BLEEP
BLEEP BLEEP
NGH...
BLEEP BLEEP
THWACK

BLEE!
...
BLEEP BLEEP BLEEP BLEEP BLEEP BLEEP
BONK
AUGUS-TINE...
YOU SURE ARE HEAVY FOR ONE PAIR OF SHOES.
I'LL HAVE TO KEEP YOU SOMEWHERE ELSE.
She named her shoes.
I THINK I FEEL A BUMP ON MY HEAD...
TMP
WHAT AWFUL LUCK...
...

HUH. IT'S CUTE.
A HEART-SHAPED MARK ON THE FOREHEAD ♡
IT'S FUNNY.
AFTER SPENDING TIME WITH SHIN MEGURO...
...EVERY-THING LOOKS BEAUTIFUL TO ME.
STARE
IT'S TOO HIGH. I CAN'T SEE IT THROUGH MY BANGS.
MORNING, MARIA!
HOW'S THE FOOT?
HIDDEN, BUT STILL BEAUTI-FUL.

ALMOST GOOD AS NEW.
IT'S BEEN A WHOLE WEEK.
THAT'S GREAT!
BUT DON'T OVERDO IT.
YOU PROBABLY WOULDN'T COMPLAIN EVEN IF IT HURT.
IF YOU NEED HELP, SAY THE WORD!
FWUFF
WON'T YOU GET SICK OF IT IF I ASK TOO MUCH?
HUH? OF COURSE NOT.
I'M AT YOUR SERVICE.
I HAVEN'T EVEN ASKED YOU TO DO ANYTHING YET.
Dummy.

UNBELIEVABLE. I GUESS SOME PEOPLE KEEP COMING TO SCHOOL NO MATTER HOW BADLY THEY HURT SOMEONE.
IT'S JUST NOT RIGHT!
NIPPACHI'S BEEN ABSENT ALL WEEK.
I WISH SHE WERE HERE.
I WONDER WHY SHE'S STAYING HOME.
I HAVE A GOOD GUESS.
THERE MUST BE SOMEONE HERE SHE REALLY DOESN'T WANT TO SEE.

SHE ISN'T HERE BECAUSE SHE DOESN'T WANT TO SEE ANYBODY.
YOU'RE ALL EQUALLY AT FAULT.
IF YOU WANT TO SEE TOMOYO KOHSAKA SO BADLY, GO GET HER.
I'M SURE SHE'S WAITING FOR YOU.
WHAT?
ARE YOU BEING SARCASTIC?!
...
COME ON, GUYS...
WHY DON'T WE ALL GO SEE HER?
WHAT FOR? SHE SHOULD GO BY HERSELF!
YUSUKE, WHY'RE YOU ALWAYS—?
THAT'S RIGHT.
ZWAK

GO BY YOURSELF, MARIA. BRING HER BACK TO SCHOOL.
TAKE SOME RESPONSIBILITY FOR YOUR ACTIONS.
BY MYSELF?
OBVIOUSLY. WHO DO YOU THINK MADE HER WANT TO STAY HOME?
YOU SAW SHE WAS VULNERABLE AND ATTACKED HER.
IF SHE DOESN'T WANT TO BE HERE, LEAVE HER ALONE.
MARIA!
YOU'RE ROTTEN TO THE CORE, YOUNG LADY.
THAT'S THE WHOLE REASON YOU HAD NO FRIENDS AT YOUR OLD SCHOOL.

TAKE NOTE, EVERYONE!
IT'S THAT KIND OF ATTITUDE THAT'LL CREATE ANOTHER NIPPACHI!
HE DOESN'T EVEN REALIZE HE'S NOT MAKING ANY SENSE.
What a wretched way to live.
FERVENT
...
ZEAL
SCRUB
SCRUB
GIRLS AND BOYS...
STUDENTS AND TEACHERS...
EVEN MY LITTLE SCAR...
THE WORLD IS FULL OF BEAUTY, ISN'T IT?
MARIA!
DON'T PAY ANY ATTENTION TO HIM.
I'LL HELP YOU CLEAN UP.
YUSUKE KANDA.

I FINALLY UNDERSTAND THE TRUE MEANING OF THE LOVELY SPIN.
HUH?
IT'S A TECHNIQUE THAT INVOLVES SEEING EVERYTHING IN THE CUTEST LIGHT POSSIBLE.
UH...
...SURE?
IS THAT IT?
FUNDAMENTALLY, YOU HAVE TO LOOK FOR THE BEAUTY IN EVERYTHING.
FOR EXAMPLE, A BLUSTERING TEACHER LIKE OURS...
...IS REALLY LIKE A BIG DOG WHO'S DESPERATELY BLUFFING SO THE PUPPIES DON'T WALK ALL OVER HIM.

IT'S STRANGE, BUT IT'S STARTING TO COME NATURALLY.
IF I SEE SOMETHING TERRIBLE AS ADORABLE INSTEAD...
...I START TO LOVE IT.
THAT'S MY CONCLUSION, ANYWAY.
BUT YOU'RE OBVIOUSLY NOT FOLLOWING ME AT ALL.
HUH?
TWITCH
NO, THAT'S NOT WHAT I—
IF I'M MISUNDER-STANDING, SAY SO.
N-NO, IT'S NOT THAT...

YOUR LOVELY SPIN IS WHATEVER WORKS FOR YOU, MARIA!
IT SOUNDS GOOD.
MAYBE I'LL TRY IT TOO.
thump
YOU'RE SO IN LOVE WITH YOUR-SELF...
...THAT YOU CAN'T EVEN BE BOTHERED TO CORRECT ME.

SHOOT...
SOMEHOW I ALWAYS END UP PUSHING YUSUKE KANDA AROUND.
amble
amble
I MAKE HIM UNCOM-FORTABLE, BUT HE'S TRYING SO HARD. IT'S CUTE.
FWOOOO...

...
drip
drip
Do you have a death wish...?
drip
drip
IF YOU KEEP THIS UP, YOU'LL DIE OF LUNG CANCER BEFORE YOU CAN KILL ANYONE.
I CAN'T BELIEVE NO ONE'S CAUGHT YOU SMOKING YET.
WHATEVER. THE TEACHERS DON'T CARE.
DONG
WHAT ABOUT CLASS?
DONG
DONG
I'M SKIPPING.
I ALWAYS GET CALLED ON IN ENGLISH.
WHY? DOES THE TEACHER HAVE IT IN FOR YOU?

I USED TO LIVE OVER-SEAS.
OHH, YOU'RE A RETURNEE?
SO HOW DO YOU EXPLAIN YOUR LACK OF COMMUNI-CATION SKILLS?
...
SMOKERS ARE LOOKED DOWN ON MORE IN OTHER COUNTRIES THAN HERE IN JAPAN.
YOUR REBEL-LIOUS NATURE HELD YOU BACK.
IT KEPT YOU FROM PICKING UP SKILLS YOU SHOULD'VE LEARNED WHILE YOU WERE ABROAD.
ABSOLUTELY RIGHT
I swear I'm gonna kill you.
A WEEK AGO YOU LOOKED HALF DEAD.
I GUESS NASTY PEOPLE RECOVER FAST.
WOULD YOU PREFER THAT I HADN'T?
IDIOT.

YOU LOOK A LOT BETTER LIKE THIS.
DO YOU MEAN THAT...
...AS IN I'M BEING TRUE TO MYSELF?

OR ARE YOU PUTTING A LOVELY SPIN ON IT?
Uh...
The...
The first one, of course! Don't be stupid!
YOU DON'T HAVE TO TAKE IT SO SERIOUSLY.
WHO'S TAKING IT SERIOUS-LY?
I WON'T SAY ANYTHING LIKE THAT AGAIN!
LIKE WHAT, SHIN MEGU-RO?
I HAD A THOUGHT.
MAYBE A LOVELY SPIN...

...IS A TYPE OF MAGIC.
HEY, YUSUKE!
WHAT'S UP WITH THOSE TWO?
English 1
THINK THEY'RE GOING OUT?
I COULDN'T TELL YOU.
WHAT? YOU DON'T KNOW?
BUT YOU'RE THE ONLY ONE WHO TALKS TO EITHER OF THEM.
MARIA PISSES ME OFF, BUT SHE'S HOT.
THAT SHIN SURE MOVES FAST.
Being gloomy doesn't slow him down.

WHO CARES...?
NIPPACHI
SANNO-CHO,
MINAMI-KU
YOKOHAMA
2-206
WHO'D TAPE TOMOYO KOHSAKA'S ADDRESS TO MY DESK? NO SUBTLETY...
MAYBE THE TEACHER?
DONG
DONG
HE'S TRYING SO HARD. IT'S ALMOST SWEET.
IT MUST LOOK BAD TO HAVE A STUDENT OUT FOR THIS LONG...
ZWAK

SHIN! WHAT'RE YOU DOING AFTER-?
CHATTER
DID YOU HEAR?
I HEARD THOSE TWO ARE...
CHATTER
SERIOUSLY? SINCE WHEN?
THAT WAS QUICK. IT'S ONLY BEEN A WEEK.
CHATTER

YUSUKE KANDA.
WHAT IS IT, MARIA?
HUH?
YOU SAID YOU'D HELP IF I NEEDED ANYTHING, RIGHT?
UM... YEAH?

COME VISIT TOMOYO KOHSAKA WITH ME.
NOT THAT I MIND, BUT...
...WHY'D YOU ASK ME TO COME WITH YOU?
YOU'RE THE ONE WHO SAID NOT TO ABANDON A FRIEND.
YOU ALSO BROUGHT HER TO THE KARAOKE PARTY.
THAT WAS A COINCIDENCE.
I THOUGHT SO.

...
BUT IT'S BE-CAUSE...
...YOU LOOKED LIKE A LOST CHILD.
YOU LOOKED LOVELY, YOU KNOW?
I COULDN'T HELP MYSELF.
WE'RE HERE.
SECOND FLOOR, APARTMENT NUMBER 6.
MARIA...
ARE YOU SAYING YOU SAW MY BAD SIDE IN A GOOD LIGHT?
DING DONG
ARE YOU SURE YOU'LL SEE ME THE SAME WAY TOMORROW?
I DON'T KNOW.
I THOUGHT SO.
SOMETHING GOOD HAPPENED TO YOU TODAY. MAYBE YOU'RE UNDER A SPELL.
DING DONG

YOU'VE GOT IT ALL WRONG, MARIA.
A LOVELY SPIN IS A MASK YOU PUT ON...
...NOT A FILTER YOU SEE THROUGH.
IT'S A SURVIVAL MECHANISM. IT LETS YOU LEAD A BEAUTIFUL LIFE.

LIAR.
HEY, IT'S LIKE I SAID.
IT DOESN'T MATTER IF IT'S TRUE OR NOT.
...
SHAK
YES?
SORRY TO DISTURB YOU! WE'RE TOMOYO'S CLASSMATES.
YUSU-KE...?
TOMOYO? IS THAT YOU?
SORRY TO DROP BY LIKE THIS...
...BUT WE REALLY WANTED TO SEE YOU.
I'D LOVE TO CHAT FOR JUST A MINUTE.
Right?
OKAY.
I'LL LET YOU IN.

Continued
in
volume 2

Greetings
TO THOSE OF YOU, WHO DON'T KNOW ME, AND TO THOSE OF YOU WHO DO...
...THANK YOU FOR READING VOLUME 1 OF A DEVIL AND HER LOVE SONG. I'M THE AUTHOR, MIYOSHI TOMORI.
It's not pronounced "Momomori."
I'm OJ, her delinquent agent.
Got a title yet?
I WANTED THE TITLE TO INCLUDE A MUSICAL REFERENCE.
SOMETHING LIKE "MARIA" OR "HALLELUJAH" OR "CANTATA...
SOMETHING HAPPY, FUN, LOVELY...
WHAT'S WRONG WITH "LOVE SONG"?
SO, THAT'S HOW IT ALL STARTED. A DEVIL AND HER LOVE SONG.
It started last year, actually...
I HOPE YOU ENJOY IT, AT LEAST A LITTLE...
So now you're making me work weekends too? Huh? You tyrant!
DELINQUENT AGENT
I HOPE TO SEE YOU AGAIN IN VOLUME 2!
Please remember me!

Please send your thoughts and comments to:

Miyoshi Tomori c/o A Devil and Her Love Song Editor
Viz Media P.O. Box 77010 San Francisco, CA 94107

可愛マリア
MARIA KAWAI

Likes music and English.
Height: 170 cm or so
Loves super-sweet foods!
Loves fluffy, white, cute, angelic things, but...
Has reddish-brown hair.
I initially modeled her after Mary Magdalene from the Bible.
(Not the Virgin Mary)

神田優介

YUSUKE KANDA

Height: 179 cm
Can run 50 meters in about six seconds.
Dyes his hair.
Doesn't like to study, but tries hard in Japanese class.
Knows a lot of kanji characters, so he does well on tests.

Height: 183 cm
His brow always looks furrowed, but that may be because of his poor eyesight. Usually wears contacts. (Single-use Acuvue)
目黒伸
SHIN MEGURO

I started on this series immediately after I finished the last one. And before I knew it, the graphic novel was being released... Everything has happened so quickly. Maria is a character you wouldn't encounter in *Hatsukare*, but nothing would please me more than if you grew to like her.

-Miyoshi Tomori

Miyoshi Tomori made her debut as a manga creator in 2001, and her previous titles include *Hatsukare* (First Boyfriend), *Tongari Root* (Square Root), and *Brass Love!!* In her spare time she likes listening to music in the bath and playing musical instruments.

A DEVIL AND HER LOVE SONG

Volume 1

Shojo Beat Edition

STORY AND ART BY
MIYOSHI TOMORI

English Adaptation/Ysabet MacFarlane
Translation/JN Productions
Touch-up Art & Lettering/Monalisa de Asis
Design/Yukiko Whitley
Editor/Amy Yu

Printed in the U.S.A.

Published by VIZ Media, LLC
P.O. Box 77010
San Francisco, CA 94107

10 9 8 7 6 5 4 3 2 1
First printing, February 2012

www.viz.com www.shojobeat.com

Heaven's Will
by Satoru Takamiya
Shojo Beat Manga
Heaven's Will
A Poem of Atonement
Complete in one volume!
Satoru Takamiya
A Frightfully Unlikely Pair
Sudou Mikuzu has a very special talent–she can see ghosts. But when she becomes a magnet for all sorts of unwelcome monsters, she calls on her new cross-dressing exorcist friend, Seto, for help. Can the mismatched duo tackle Sudou's supernatural problems?
Find out in the Heaven's Will manga—available now!
On sale at www.shojobeat.com
Also available at your local bookstore and comic store.
viz media
www.viz.com
ratings.viz.com
Shojo Beat

Can love trump a cursed life?
Sawako's a shy, lonely, pure-hearted student who just happens to look like the scary girl in a famous horror movie! But when she manages to befriend the most popular boy in school, will her frightful reputation scare off her best chance for love?
kimi ni todoke
From Me to You
By Karuho Shiina
kimi ni todoke
From Me to You
Karuho Shiina
Find out in the Kimi ni Todoke manga—
BUY YOURS TODAY!
Winner of the 2008
Kodansha Manga Award
(shojo category)
On sale at www.shojobeat.com
Also available at your local bookstore or comic store
Shojo Beat
MANGA from the HEART
RATED T FOR TEEN
ratings.viz.com
viz media
www.viz.com
KIMI NI TODOKE © 2005 Karuho Shiina/SHUEISHA Inc.

love★com
By Aya Nakahara
Shojo Beat Manga
love★com
Love★Com
Lovely ★ Complex
Aya Nakahara
1
Class clowns Risa and Ôtani join forces to find love!
Manga available now
On sale at www.shojobeat.com
Also available at your local bookstore and comic store
LOVE★COM © 2001 by Aya Nakahara/SHUEISHA Inc.
Shojo Beat
RATED T TEEN
ratings.viz.com
viz media
www.viz.com